D0257362

PASSPORT TO DELICIOUS AND SIMPLE HOLIDAY EATING

PASSPORT TO DELICIOUS AND SIMPLE HOLIDAY EATING

Diana Johnson

Library of Congress Control Number: 2016901197
ISBN: Hardcover   978-1-4990-9810-5
               Softcover   978-1-4990-9809-9
               eBook   978-1-4990-9808-2

Print information available on the last page.

Rev. date: 03/18/2016

To order additional copies of this book, contact:
Xlibris
0-800-443-678
www.Xlibris.co.nz
Orders@Xlibris.co.nz
729346

CONTENTS

PREFACE

Here are some quick, easy, and delicious recipes for everyone to have fun with on holidays, whether at home, at the holiday house, or further afield.

I have included lots of delicious dishes that will take as little time as possible to prepare with limited ingredients and few utensils, especially for holiday eating.

Perhaps the family have brought you a trout that you don't know what to do with, or maybe the area that you are visiting is abundant with fresh fruit, wine, seafood, or fresh vegetables, which you'd love to make the most of.

I have included dishes that make the best out of some of those fresh ingredients.

I have also tried, wherever possible, not to need to weigh ingredients.

I have also set up these recipes in a passport form to help keep your passport safe.

If you are in a position where you are asked for your passport by someone questionable, (not when you're going through customs though), just push this book into their hands. You may lose these recipes, but just contact us to purchase another one.

BREAKFASTS

Traditional Muesli

6 cups rolled oats
1 cup wheat flakes
1 cup coconut
1 cup unprocessed bran
1 cup wheatgerm
1/4 cup sesame seeds
1 teaspoon cinnamon
1 cup vegetable oil
1 cup honey
1/4 cup chopped dried apricots
1/4 cup chopped dried pineapple
1 cup mixed dried fruit
1 tablespoon candied lemon peel

In a large roasting dish, mix together oats, wheat flakes, coconut, bran, wheatgerm, sesame seeds, and cinnamon.

Heat together the vegetable oil and honey, and add to the roasting dish. Mix well with the dry ingredients.

Bake at 130 °C for 1 hour until crunchy.

When cool, add the dried apricots, dried pineapple, mixed dried fruit, and the candied lemon peel.

This keeps well in an airtight container.

DIPS AND STARTERS

Guacamole

2 mashed avocados
1 chopped tomato
1/2 chopped red onion
1 clove finely chopped or crushed garlic (optional)
juice of 1/2 lemon
1/2 teaspoon Tabasco sauce

Mix all ingredients together.

Season with salt and pepper.
Serve as a dip with corn chips, bread, or sticks of carrot and celery or with Mexican dishes.

Nectarine Salsa

1 nectarine, finely chopped
1 small onion, peeled and finely chopped
1/4 cup chopped walnuts
1 tablespoon cider vinegar
1 or 2 fresh green chillies, chopped (optional)
To Serve
Crusty bread

Combine all ingredients.

Serve with crusty bread.

BREADS

Mafia Bread

2 cups plain yogurt
3 cups self-raising flour
1 packet onion soup

Mix all together and knead. Place on a greased and floured baking tray. Bake at 180 °C for 20-25 minutes.

This is a great lunch bread, especially for picnics.

No-Knead Bread

3 cups wholemeal (or white) flour
1 teaspoon powdered yeast
1 1/4 teaspoon salt
375 mls warm water

Dissolve yeast and salt in warm water.

Pour flour into a mixing bowl.

Pour water-and-yeast mixture into flour, and combine with a wooden spoon.

Cover with cling wrap, and leave in a warm place for 2 hours until risen.

Preheat oven to 200 °C.

Gently shape into balls if making buns or into a loaf shape and place on baking paper on an oven tray.

Diana Johnson

Cover again and let the dough rise for a further 20-30 minutes.

Cook for approximately 25 minutes until golden brown.

Pikelets

1 cup self-raising flour
1/4 teaspoon salt
1 egg
1/4 cup sugar
3/4 cup milk

To Serve
Raspberry jam
Whipped cream
Or
Slices of smoked salmon
Sour cream
Chopped chives or capers

Sift the flour and salt, or stir with a whisk.

In another bowl, beat the egg and sugar until thick, and add to dry ingredients with the milk.

Mix until combined, but don't over-mix. Heat a non-stick frying pan, and grease with butter. Drop mixture from a tablespoon on to the hot pan. Turn over when bubbles begin to burst. Cook the second side until golden brown.

Serve with raspberry jam and whipped cream or as finger food by topping with slices of smoked salmon, sour cream, and chopped chives or capers.

ENTRÉES AND LUNCHES

Prawn or Seafood Cocktail
with Seafood Sauce

1/2 cup mayonnaise
1/2 cup whipped cream or sour cream or Greek-style yogurt
1 tablespoon tomato sauce
1 teaspoon curry powder
juice from 1/2 lemon
pinch of cayenne pepper

Mix all ingredients except whipped cream or yogurt. When ready to serve, fold in the cream or yogurt, and spoon over the cooked prawns or seafood: mussels, shrimps, prawns, crabs, etc. Serve in a lettuce leaf or over salad greens in glasses or small bowls.

This recipe is for that special occasion when fresh seafood is readily available directly from the fishing boats if your holiday is by the sea, or from the seafood department of supermarkets.

Antipasto

This is a platter of food for the centre of the table for all to pick from and a great way to put food in front of hungry people in a few minutes. Antipasto can deal with appetites of all sizes and varied dietary needs. It can be varied daily, giving a variety of choices and is ideal for lunch or starter.

Suggestions are: smoked salmon or seared tuna with lemon and capers or caper berries, stuffed or hard-boiled eggs, dips, salamis, cold meats, English pork pies (eaten cold) with mustards and chutneys, bacon-and-egg pie, cooked chicken with cranberry sauce, cheeses, gherkins, pickles, frittata* or self-crusting pie* served warm or cold, spicy nuts*, lettuce leaves, tomatoes, cucumber, olives, pickled mushrooms*, beetroot, and baby corn cobs. Include a jar of feta and chilli*.

Serve with lots of crusty bread, crackers, and dressings.

Some recipes for your platter can be made before you leave home to take with you, or just to keep in the cupboard for those unexpected visitors.

- *These are recipes available in this book.

Feta and Chilli

130g diced feta cheese
5 roasted garlic cloves*
1 teaspoon mixed peppercorns
A few drops of Tabasco sauce
olive oil to cover

In a jar, layer diced feta, roasted garlic cloves, mixed peppercorns, and Tabasco sauce. Cover in oil.

Seal and refrigerate.

(Garlic cloves can be roasted in the microwave by taking 1 or more heads of garlic. Cut the tops off to expose the garlic cloves and place in a microwave bowl. Sprinkle with a little olive oil and salt and pepper, adding 1 1/2 tablespoons of water or wine.

Cover and cook at 50 per cent power for 3 minutes.

If the cloves are not soft, cook for a further 3 minutes and then 1 minute at a time until cooked.

Pickled Mushrooms

1 kg small button mushrooms
2 cups cider vinegar
1 teaspoon salt
2 cups water

2 tablespoons mustard seeds
2 tablespoons peppercorns
4-5 garlic cloves or shallots
4-5 bay leaves
1 sprig thyme
1 sprig rosemary

Into a pot place the mushrooms, vinegar, salt and water. Bring to the boil and simmer for 10 minutes.

Drain the mushrooms well, wrap in a tea towel, and leave overnight. The following morning, into a preserving jar, layer mushrooms alternately with the mustard seeds, peppercorns, garlic cloves or shallots, bay leaves, thyme and rosemary.

Cover with olive oil, and keep in a cool place for up to 3 months.

Spicy Nuts

1 tablespoon vegetable oil
1 tablespoon sugar
pinch of turmeric
140 g blanched almonds
70 g raw cashews
1 tablespoon coarse sea salt
1/2 teaspoon garam masala
1/4 teaspoon chilli powder

Diana Johnson

Cook all ingredients in a pan over medium heat, tossing frequently until golden.

Remove from the pan, cool, and serve with a little extra sea salt.

Prawn Tartlets and Spicy Mango Chutney with Coriander

3-4 sheets Mountain Bread or tortillas

1 thumb-sized piece fresh ginger, chopped
3 cloves garlic, crushed
1 teaspoon cumin
1 teaspoon paprika
1 tablespoon butter
1 tablespoon vegetable oil
200 g small cooked prawns
2 tablespoons plain yogurt
1 tablespoon lime juice
Garnish
Fresh coriander
To serve
Spicy Mango Chutney with Coriander

Preheat oven to 200 °C.
Grease 24 muffin pans.
Cut rounds of mountain bread or tortillas to fit pans.
Bake 3-4 minutes until crisp.
These can be made ahead and kept in an airtight container.
For the filling, heat oil and butter in a pan.
Fry ginger, garlic, cumin, and paprika.
Remove from heat, add yogurt and lime juice, and mix in the prawns.
Spoon the prawn mixture into shells, and garnish with coriander.
Serve with spicy mango chutney with coriander.

Spicy Mango Chutney with Coriander

1/4 cup mango chutney
1/2 cup chopped coriander leaves
1 large red chilli, seeds removed and chopped finely
1 tablespoon lime juice
1/2 teaspoon ground cumin

Process all of the ingredients until smooth.

Chill in a covered container in the fridge.

This will keep for 1-2 days.

Cocktail Sausages

1 kg small breakfast sausages
2 tablespoons sesame oil
2 tablespoons soya sauce
150 g honey

Preheat oven to 180 °C.

Place sausages in a flat roasting dish lined with foil.

Mix together the sesame oil, soya sauce, and honey, and pour over the sausages.

Cook for 20-30 minutes.

Smoked Salmon with Mandarins

150g smoked salmon slices or pieces
1 avocado, peeled, stone removed, and sliced
1/2 lemon

1 small can mandarin segments, drained
1 tablespoon chopped walnuts
4 sprigs of parsley

To Serve
Seafood Sauce

For this easy entrée, arrange slices or pieces of smoked salmon on serving plates. Add the sliced avocado and squeeze over the lemon to stop the avocado from browning. Add the drained mandarin segments, the chopped walnuts, and some parsley to decorate.

Use the Seafood Sauce for a tasty sauce to add to this dish.

Simple Sorbet

1 can of pears or peaches
Cointreau or fruit liqueur to taste
pinch of ground cloves or cinnamon

Place the can in the freezer the night before it's needed.

Just before serving remove the can from freezer and run under hot tap to loosen the frozen fruit. Cut the top and base from the can and push the fruit from the into the food processor or kitchen whizz.

Break up roughly and whizz, adding Cointreau or fruit liqueur, ground cloves, or cinnamon. Serve in tall glasses.

Ploughman's Lunch

crusty bread
butter
cheeses

pickles
English pork pies (serve cold)

Arrange on a board or platter or as individual servings.
Serve with a mug of hot soup.

Spicy Thai Patties

2 x 85 g cans of spicy Thai salmon
3 cups mashed potatoes
1/2 cup flour
1 egg
1 spring onion, finely sliced
2 tablespoons coriander
2 tablespoons finely chopped red pepper
To Serve
Sweet chilli sauce

Mix all ingredients, adding extra flour if the mixture is too wet.
Roll into balls, flatten, coat with flour, and fry evenly.
Serve with sweet chilli sauce.

Frittata

6 eggs
1 cup milk
1/2 cup self-raising flour
2 cups sliced mushrooms
1 cup chopped ham
2 cups peeled and sliced potatoes
2 tablespoons chopped parsley

Grease an ovenproof lasagne dish. Mix all ingredients together and
pour into the dish.

Diana Johnson

Bake at 200 °C for 20-25 minutes.

The true Spanish frittata, as I have tasted in Spanish homes, is made with onions, sliced potatoes, and sliced red peppers (optional), fried gently until almost cooked. Then the whisked eggs are added, seasoned, and either put under the grill to cook the top, or, when the base is cooked, a plate is placed on top of the frying pan, inverted and slid, back into the pan to cook the other side which is not as easy as it sounds.

This frittata can be served hot or cold or added to your platter.

This is another variation, which is great to take on a picnic or as a lunch dish. Leave out the ham and add some sliced red peppers, and you'll have a great vegetarian dish.

Self-Crusting Pie

4 eggs, beaten
1 1/2 cups grated tasty cheese
1 small onion, chopped
6 rashers of rindless bacon, chopped
1/2 cup self-raising flour
1 1/2 cups milk
1/4 cup chopped parsley
salt and freshly ground black pepper to taste
2 cups chopped peppers, mushrooms, cherry tomatoes, courgettes, corn, peas, beans, grated pumpkin, etc. (your choice)

Preheat oven to 180 °C. Grease or spray a medium to large lasagne dish.

Mix all ingredients in a bowl.

Pour into prepared dish, and bake for 40-45 minutes until set and golden brown. Cut into thick slices.

Can be eaten hot or cold.

Pizza Base with Toppings
(no yeast)

1 small cup self-raising flour
(or plain flour plus 1 small teaspoon baking powder)
1 large tablespoon oil or butter
1/2 teaspoon salt
large pinch of oregano
milk or water to mix to a firm dough

For the base, rub the oil or butter into the flour and add the salt. Mix with milk or water.

Knead lightly and roll out or press into a pizza tray.

Toppings

5 tablespoons pasta sauce
1 small onion, chopped
2 medium tomatoes, sliced
1/2 cup of tasty cheese, grated
½ cup mozzarella cheese, grated
1 tablespoon oregano, chopped
Salt and pepper to taste

Spread the pasta sauce over the base and arrange the onion, tomatoes, and cheeses on top. Sprinkle with oregano and season with salt and pepper.

Diana Johnson

Additional toppings

Strips of bacon, salami, oysters, anchovies, pimento, drained crushed pineapple or mushrooms, can be added according to taste.

Cook for 30 minutes at 200 °C.

Mushroom Risotto
(microwave)

1 cup Arborio rice
3 cups water
5-6 brown flat mushrooms, chopped
1 tablespoon olive oil
1 1/2 teaspoons vegetable stock powder
2 tablespoons (extra) olive oil or butter
freshly grated Parmesan cheese

Place everything except the extra oil or butter, and cheese into a large, deep microwave bowl with tight-fitting lid.

Cook on high heat for 20 minutes. Remove from the microwave.

Stir and let stand for 5 minutes to allow the remaining liquid to be absorbed.

Add the extra oil (or butter, to be more traditional). Mix thoroughly and serve with Parmesan cheese.

Instead of mushrooms, use chorizo sausage cut into slices and fried, adding green peas at the end of the frying.

Homestyle Baked Beans

150 g speck bacon, cut into fine batons
2 garlic cloves
2 brown onions, sliced
2 tablespoons tomato paste
2 tablespoons brown sugar
1 teaspoon smoked paprika
1 cup chicken stock
1 teaspoon hot English mustard
2 teaspoons molasses
2 tablespoons apple cider vinegar
2 x 400 g cans cannellini beans, drained and rinsed
1/4 bunch parsley leaves, chopped
salt and freshly ground black pepper to taste

Sauté bacon until golden and crisp. Add the onions and garlic, and cook for 2 minutes. Stir in the tomato paste, sugar, and paprika.

Cook briefly until sugar begins to stick to the base of the pan.

Add stock, mustard, molasses, and vinegar. Simmer for 2 minutes.

Add beans, and cook gently with the lid ajar for 10 minutes. Fold in parsley. Season, and serve on grilled sourdough.

How to Cook Perfect Rice Every Time

2 cups long grain rice
Cold water for rinsing and cooking
1 teaspoon salt

Place rice in a medium-sized saucepan.

Diana Johnson

Rinse by adding cold water, stirring and pouring off and repeating until the water runs clear.

Add cold water until the depth of the water comes to your first knuckle when touching the top of the rice.

Add salt. Heat until the rice comes to the boiling point.

Turn off heat and place lid firmly on the rice and leave while you prepare the rest of your meal.

This method of cooking rice was shown to me by a Thai student who stayed with us a few years ago.

Corn Arepas with Chicken and Mayonnaise Filling

2 1/2 cups warm water
2 cups cornmeal flour
1 teaspoon salt

Chicken-Mayo Filling
2 chicken breasts
1 onion finely chopped
2 peppercorns
1 bay leaf
2 garlic cloves
2 stoned, peeled, and sliced avocadoes
2 tablespoons chopped coriander leaves
1 tablespoon lemon or lime juice
1/2 teaspoon coarse salt

cracked pepper
1-2 chopped chillies (optional)
2 tablespoons mayonnaise

For the corn arepas, pour water into a bowl with the salt. Slowly add cornmeal, and knead with hands. Once combined, let the mixture rest for 2 minutes, then knead until smooth.

Roll into balls about the size of a billiard ball. Flatten and moisten the edges.

Heat grill plate to medium heat. Grease with oil.

Cook 3-4 minutes each side until golden brown.

Preheat oven to 200 °C, and bake for 7-10 minutes. Arepas are ready when they sound hollow when tapped.

For the chicken filling, place chicken, onion, peppercorns, bay leaf, and garlic cloves into a large saucepan. Cover with water. Bring to the boil, and simmer for approximately 15 minutes or until chicken breasts are cooked through.

Drain, cool, and shred the chicken. Mix with 2 tablespoons mayonnaise or to taste.

Add the avocado, coriander, and lemon or lime juice to chicken-and-mayo mixture. Season with salt, black pepper, and chillies. Carefully mix all together.

Slice open the arepas, and fill with chicken-and-avocado mixture.

These delicious cornmeal patties can be grilled, baked, boiled, or fried and stuffed.

THE MAIN COURSE

Stir-Fried Beef and Pak Choi in Sauce

500 g rump steak, sliced thinly
3 heads of pak choi
1 clove garlic, chopped
1 dessertspoon grated ginger
vegetable oil for frying

Sauce
zest of 1 orange and 1/2 juice
3 tablespoons sherry
2 tablespoons soya sauce
2 tablespoons hoisin sauce
1 tablespoon cornflour

To Serve
Rice or noodles

Whisk together the orange juice, sherry, soya sauce, hoisin sauce, and cornflour.

Lightly fry the garlic and freshly grated ginger in vegetable oil without browning.

Add sliced beef and stir.

Add 3 heads of pak choi cut into quarters lengthwise.

Cook for approximately 3 minutes.

Add sauce and cook further for 3 minutes and serve with rice or noodles.

Beef Stroganoff

1 kg rump steak, sliced thinly
2 tablespoons oil
1 sliced onion
1 clove garlic, crushed
1 cup mushrooms, sliced
1 can mushroom soup
1 cup sour cream
2 tablespoons tomato sauce
2 teaspoons Worcestershire sauce

To Serve
Ribbon noodles or rice

In a frying pan or wok, brown the steak in the oil.

Add the onion, garlic, and mushrooms, and cook for a further 5 minutes, stirring to cook evenly.

Combine the mushroom soup, sour cream, tomato sauce, and Worcestershire sauce, and add to the steak mixture.

Heat through, and serve with ribbon noodles or rice.

Tuscan Beef with Pasta

4 tablespoons olive oil
1 onion, peeled and finely diced
2 cloves garlic, peeled and crushed
500 g lean minced beef
1 teaspoon each of allspice, cinnamon, whole cloves, and paprika
2-3 bay leaves
130 g tomato paste

500-g jar of prepared pasta sauce
1 tablespoon beef stock powder
150 g smoked bacon, cooked and diced
dash of Worcestershire sauce

To Serve
250 g spaghetti or fettuccini
2-3 diced fresh tomatoes
chopped herbs: basil, parsley, or chives
Parmesan cheese
basil pesto

Heat the oil in a frying pan, and brown onion, garlic, beef, and spices over high heat. Add bay leaves, tomato paste, pasta sauce, stock powder, bacon, and Worcestershire sauce.

Stir until mixed well. Reduce heat and gently simmer uncovered for 30 minutes, stirring occasionally.

Cook the pasta until al dente, drain and toss together with the diced tomatoes and chopped herbs. Serve the meat sauce over hot pasta accompanied by Parmesan cheese and basil pesto.

Chilli con Carne
(microwave)

500 g minced steak
1 onion, chopped
1 clove garlic, crushed
2 teaspoons chilli powder
300 g can tomato soup
440-g can red kidney beans (or chilli beans for extra heat)

To Serve
Cooked rice or pasta
Grated tasty cheese
Sour cream
Green salad
Or
Taco shells
Chopped tomatoes
Shredded lettuce

Place minced onion, garlic, chilli powder, and tomato soup in a casserole, and mix well.

Cook on medium heat for 10 minutes.

Stir halfway through cooking.

Add beans.

Stir well and cook further on medium heat for 10 minutes.

Serve with rice or pasta, grated tasty cheese, sour cream with green salad, or in taco shells with chopped tomatoes and shredded lettuce.

Chicken Schnitzel

8 chicken breasts
1 cup of Arrowroot flour
1/2 cup corn flour
1 teaspoon garlic powder
1 teaspoon paprika
4 eggs
squeeze of lemon juice
4 garlic cloves, crushed

Diana Johnson

2 lemons sliced
4 small cubes of butter
½ cup white wine
1 ½ cups chicken stock
Squeeze lemon juice

Dressing
1 shallot, grated
salt to taste
2 teaspoons Dijon mustard
3 tablespoons white wine vinegar
3/4 cup olive oil

To Serve
assorted lettuce leaves
1 tablespoon tarragon leaves, chopped
1 tablespoon parsley, chopped
1 lemon, sliced

Pound the chicken breasts in freezer bags, and stack them in the freezer until ready to use.

Defrost, and season with salt and pepper.

Mix the Arrowroot flour, corn flour, garlic powder, and paprika together.

In a separate bowl, beat together the eggs, lemon juice, and garlic cloves.

Dip chicken breasts one at a time into the flour mixture then egg, and back into flour mixture. Fry on each side. Put to one side, and dip slices of lemon into flour, and fry. Dip 4 small cubes of butter into the flour for thickening the gravy.

Deglaze the pan with the white wine and add the floured small cubes of butter. Add 1 1/2 cups chicken stock and a squeeze of lemon juice and boil for 3 minutes.

For the dressing, mix the shallot, salt, Dijon mustard, wine vinegar, and olive oil together in a screw-top jar, and shake to combine.

Serve the chicken topped with gravy, then a salad of assorted lettuce, tarragon leaves, and parsley with lemon slices on the side.

Serve dressing separately.

Chicken Goulash

1 cooked, boned chicken, cut into small pieces
1 small can pineapple pieces, drained
2 packets mushroom soup mix
3 teaspoons curry powder
1 small can creamed corn
1 cup cream
2 cups milk

Mix all ingredients together, and cook in a casserole dish at 180 °C for one hour.

Serve with rice.

Stir-Fried Chicken and Cashew Nuts with Noodles

2 packets instant chicken noodles, prepared and drained as per packet instructions (using the flavour sachets), and set aside
2 teaspoons olive oil
400 g skinless chicken breasts, thinly sliced
250 g green beans, halved (or other green vegetables, such as celery, sliced)
1 red capsicum, seeds removed, sliced
2 tablespoons sweet chilli sauce
1/2 cup plain cashew nuts

Diana Johnson

Heat the oil in a frying pan.

Cook chicken until brown and cooked through.

Add green beans or celery and red capsicum.

Cook, stirring, for 3 minutes.

Add drained noodles and sweet chilli sauce, and cook further for 2 minutes, stirring.

Stir in cashew nuts, and serve immediately.

This recipe serves 4.

Sweet-and-Sour Stir-Fried Chicken

2 tablespoons oil
750 g chicken thigh fillets, sliced
Sauce
220 g can pineapple pieces drained reserving syrup
2 teaspoons light soya sauce
2 tablespoons tomato sauce
1 tablespoon sugar
1 tablespoon malt vinegar
1 tablespoon lemon juice
1 teaspoon grated fresh ginger
1 tablespoon maize cornflour
3/4 cup water
1 red pepper, chopped
2 sticks celery, sliced
2 green shallots, chopped
310 g can mandarin segments, drained

To Serve
Cooked rice or noodles

Heat oil in wok or pan, and fry chicken in batches until lightly brown and cooked through.

Drain on absorbent paper, and keep warm.

Drain excess oil from pan.

For the sauce, add the reserved pineapple syrup, sauces, sugar, vinegar, juice, and ginger together with the blended corn flour and water.

Stir over heat until mixture boils and thickens. Add pineapple, pepper, and celery. Cook for 1 minute.

Add chicken, shallots, and mandarins, and stir until heated through.

Serve over rice or noodles.

This recipe serves six.

Tandoori Chicken Kebabs with Couscous and Tzatziki

1 tray of tandoori kebabs

Couscous
1 cup couscous
1/2 cup chopped pistachio nuts
1/2 cup chopped parsley
2 tablespoons chopped oregano

Dressing
1/4 cup olive oil
zest and juice of 1 lemon
1 tablespoon sweet chilli sauce
salt and pepper to taste

Place couscous in a bowl, and add 1 cup boiling water.

Cover and allow to steam for 5 minutes.

Fluff up the couscous with a fork.

Stir in the nuts and herbs.

Mix dressing ingredients together.

Pour over couscous and toss well.

Grill the tandoori chicken skewers on each side on a BBQ or in a frying pan.

Tzatziki
1 small cucumber, deseeded and diced
1 clove garlic, peeled and crushed
1/4 cup finely chopped mint
1/4 cup finely chopped fresh dill
1 cup unsweetened yogurt
salt and white pepper to taste

Mix tzatziki ingredients together, and season to taste.

Serve cooked kebabs on the couscous salad topped with tzatziki sauce.

Spaghetti with Meatballs

500 g minced pork
1/2 finely chopped medium onion
salt and pepper to taste,
1 tablespoon each of chopped parsley and oregano
440 g can or jar of pasta sauce
250 g spaghetti
1 teaspoon salt

To Serve
grated tasty cheese
sour cream
green salad
crusty bread

Mix minced pork, onion, salt and pepper, and fresh herbs, and roll into balls about the size of a walnut.

Brown in a little oil in a deep-sided pan.

Add pasta sauce.

Meanwhile, cook the spaghetti in a large saucepan of boiling water with 1 teaspoon salt until al dente.

Drain and serve with meatballs and sauce, grated tasty cheese, sour cream, a green salad, and crusty bread.

Meat Loaf

2 teaspoons oil
1 onion, chopped
3 cloves garlic, chopped

3 cups fresh breadcrumbs
800 g minced pork
2 eggs, whisked
1 tablespoon tomato sauce
1 tablespoon each of chives and parsley, chopped
2 teaspoons sweet chilli sauce

Sauce
250 g sour cream
2 tablespoons grainy mustard
2 tablespoons chilli sauce

Mix oil, onion, garlic, breadcrumbs, minced pork, eggs, tomato sauce, herbs, and sweet chilli sauce, and press into a loaf tin or make into individual rolls and wrap with a slice of bacon.

Bake at 200 °C for 30-35 minutes.

To make the sauce, mix together the sour cream, grainy mustard, and chilli sauce. Serve with the meat loaf.

This meat loaf is great cold or hot, whatever the weather.

Spanish Paella

1 onion
1 clove garlic
5 tablespoons oil
2 cups long-grain rice
2 1/2 cups chicken stock
1/2 cooked, boned chicken, cut into pieces
1 can sweet red pepper
3-4 peeled and chopped tomatoes
1 can mussels

1/4 teaspoon saffron
250 g fresh shrimps or prawns or scallops
or a mixture (can use frozen)
250 g peas (can use frozen)
1 small jar stuffed olives

Chop the onion, and finely chop the garlic.

Fry in oil in a large pan with a lid until transparent.

Add the rice, and cook, stirring for 4 minutes.

Pour in the hot chicken stock.

Cover with a lid or foil and cook until almost tender for 7-10 minutes.

Add more stock if necessary.

Slice the red pepper.

Add all other ingredients, including tomatoes and mixed seafood.

Cook until everything is heated through.

Paella should be served fairly dry.

Serve with a green salad.

This is a Spanish favourite and varies in different areas of the country and is great for any seafood you may have. Preparation and cooking time is 30 minutes.

Diana Johnson

Thai Chicken Curry

1 tablespoon olive oil
4 skinless chicken breasts, sliced into 2 cm pieces
25 g cashew nuts
1 heaped teaspoon red curry paste
3 capsicums (1 green, 1 red, and 1 yellow), sliced into strips
2 red onions, sliced
2 cloves garlic, finely sliced
1/2 cup soya sauce
1 dessertspoon honey
1 cup fresh coriander, finely chopped
1 teaspoon chopped or grated fresh ginger
4 green ends of spring onion, finely sliced
1/2 cup sliced canned bamboo shoots
1/2 cup cooked long-grain rice per person

Pour olive oil into a wok or large pan. Add chicken, and toss until sealed.

Add nuts, curry paste, capsicum, onion, garlic, and ginger. Toss all ingredients together until chicken is cooked through.

Reduce heat slightly, and add soya sauce and honey.

Simmer until reduced and slightly thickened. Stir through coriander, spring onion, and bamboo shoots.

Serve on hot cooked rice.

Sweet-and-Sour Pork

1 can pineapple chunks (2 1/4 cups), drain and reserve the juice
1 kg lean pork, cut into strips
3/4 cup green pepper, sliced into strips

1/4 cup thinly sliced onion
1/4 cup brown sugar
2 tablespoons cornflour
1/4 cup vinegar
1 tablespoon soya sauce
1/2 teaspoon salt

Brown the pork in a pan in a little hot oil, add 1/4 cup water, and simmer until tender.

Mix together in a saucepan, the brown sugar, cornflour, vinegar,

soya sauce, salt and combine with the juice from the pineapple. Heat, stirring until thick, and add to the pork. Allow to stand for 10 minutes.

Add pineapple, green-pepper strips, and sliced onions. Cook for 3-4 minutes.

Serve over noodles or rice.

This is quick and easy but delicious.

PASTA

Fettuccine with Chicken and Bacon

250 g fettuccine or spaghetti

1 tablespoon butter
3 chicken breasts or thigh fillets, thinly sliced
2 rashers rindless bacon, finely chopped
6 spring onions or shallots, chopped
300 mls cream or yogurt
1 chicken stock cube
1/2 cup grated Parmesan cheese
ground pepper

To Serve
extra grated Parmesan cheese
green salad
crusty bread

Boil the pasta in salted water until al dente.

Heat butter in a large pan.

Add the chicken and bacon and cook until chicken is golden.

Lower heat, and add chopped onions or shallots, cream or yogurt, chicken stock cube and Parmesan cheese.

Cook for 10 minutes, stirring until thickened.

Additions such as chopped mushrooms and chopped red peppers can be added after frying the bacon and chicken.

Drain the pasta, and stir through sauce, using a little of the pasta water to thin the sauce if needed.

Serve with salad and crusty bread and extra grated Parmesan cheese.

Honey-and-Mustard-Chicken Pasta Salad

300 g macaroni or other small pasta

3 tablespoons mayonnaise
1 heaped teaspoon wholegrain mustard
1 teaspoon clear honey
300 g cooked chicken, boned and cut into pieces
4 spring onions, sliced, or 1/2 red onion, sliced
small bunch basil leaves, torn roughly
4 tomatoes, quartered then cut into halves

Boil the pasta until al dente, and cool under running water.

Mix the mayo, mustard, and honey and loosen with a little of the pasta water to make the consistency of double cream.

Add pasta, chicken, onions, basil, and tomatoes.

Season to taste then gently mix.

FISH DISHES

Prawn Salad

2 cups small prawns, cooked
1/2 packet vermicelli thread noodles, soaked
in boiling water for 5 minutes
1 cup of sugar snap peas, blanched by pouring
boiling water over them and drained
handful of bean sprouts
2 chopped spring onions

Dressing
1 tablespoon grated ginger
1 clove garlic, chopped finely (or use a garlic press)
1 long red chilli, seeded and chopped
1 teaspoon sugar
juice of 1 lime
2 tablespoons fish sauce
(or 2 tablespoons soya sauce and 1 tablespoons wine vinegar)
2 teaspoons sesame oil

Mix together the prawns, noodles, peas, bean sprouts, and spring onions.

In a separate bowl, mix together the dressing ingredients: ginger, garlic, chilli, sugar, lime juice, fish sauce (or soya sauce and wine vinegar), and sesame oil.

When ready to serve, pour the dressing over the prawn-and-vermicelli mixture.

Prawn Omelettes

8 eggs, beaten with whisk or electric beater
salt and pepper
4 medium mushrooms, chopped finely
4 shallots, finely chopped
1 stick of celery, finely chopped
250 g shelled and chopped prawns
250 g bean sprouts

Sauce
1 cup water
1 tablespoon cornflour
2 teaspoons chicken stock
1 teaspoon sugar
2 teaspoons soya sauce
salt

Season the eggs with salt and pepper.

Fry chopped mushrooms for one minute, and add to egg mixture.

Add shallots, celery, prawns, and bean sprouts.

For the sauce, stir water, cornflour, chicken stock, sugar, soya sauce and salt together, and microwave on high heat for 3 minutes or until thick.

Stir after each minute.

Pour oil into medium-sized frying pan to just cover the base, and cook the omelettes until firm.

Turn them over, and cook the other side.

Stack on a warm plate while cooking the remainder.

Diana Johnson

To serve, stack 2 omelettes on each plate, and spoon sauce over them.

This recipe serves 4.

Chilli-and-Prawn Chow Mein

24 large prawns, peeled, deveined, and halved
1/2 teaspoon salt
1/2 teaspoon chilli powder

1-1 1/2 tablespoons vegetable oil
3 shallots, finely diced
3 cm piece of ginger, finely chopped
1 clove garlic, finely sliced
200 g ribbon-cut egg noodles (or rice noodles),
cooked as per packet directions
1 teaspoon caster sugar
2 tablespoons Chinese rice wine
1 tablespoon soya sauce
2 tablespoons oyster sauce
2-3 spring onions, sliced
large handful coriander, chopped

Rub prawns with salt and chilli powder.

Cover and refrigerate while you prepare the rest of the chow mein.

Heat oil in a wok.

Add shallots and ginger, and stir-fry for 1-2 minutes.

Add prawns and garlic, and stir-fry further for 2-3 minutes or until almost pink all over.

Stir in prepared noodles, and toss to coat in the oil, adding a little extra if necessary.

Combine the sugar, rice wine, soya sauce, and oyster sauce in a small bowl.

Add to pan, toss to combine, and bring back to the boil.

Most of the liquid will be absorbed.

Toss the spring onions through.

Remove from heat, and toss the coriander through.

Serve immediately.

This recipe serves 3-4.

Fish Tagine with Herb Couscous

4 fish fillets (snapper or blue cod), halved crosswise
2 tablespoons Moroccan spice mix
2 tablespoons olive oil
1 large brown onion, sliced
3 cloves garlic, crushed
1 medium lemon, sliced thinly
12 green olives, pitted
1 cup salt-reduced chicken stock
1 teaspoon sugar

Garnish
2 tablespoons chopped coriander leaves

Herb Couscous
1 cup couscous
1 cup boiling water
1/2 cup firmly packed coriander leaves

To Serve
Steamed zucchini

Preheat oven to 200 °C.

Place fish-and-spice mixture in a large bowl, and toss to coat fish.

Heat half the oil in a large flameproof oven dish over medium heat. Cook onion and garlic, stirring until soft.

Remove from pan and set aside.

Heat remaining oil in pan, and cook fish in batches until brown on both sides.

Return onion mixture to pan, and add lemon slices, olives, stock, and sugar.

Bring to the boil. Transfer the pan to the oven.

Bake uncovered for 10 minutes or until fish is just cooked through.

Remove fish from oven. Sprinkle with coriander.

For the herb couscous, combine couscous with boiling water in a medium heatproof bowl.

Cover and let stand for 5 minutes until liquid is absorbed.

Fluff with fork occasionally.

Stir in coriander leaves.

Serve fish tagine with herb couscous and steamed zucchini slices.

Seafood Marinara
(microwave)

250 g scallops
250 g prawns, shelled and deveined
1 squid, cleaned and sliced
(could use frozen seafood)

2 tablespoons butter
1 clove garlic, crushed
2 tomatoes, peeled and chopped
1 tablespoon tomato paste
1/4 cup white wine
1 teaspoon dried basil
pepper to taste
chopped parsley

To Serve

300g pasta Fusilli or similar
green salad

Place cleaned seafood in a 1-litre casserole, and set aside.

Place butter and garlic in a small dish, and cook on high heat for 1 minute.

Add garlic, tomatoes, tomato paste, white wine, basil, pepper and chopped parsley.

Diana Johnson

Cook on high heat for 5 minutes.

Puree tomato mixture in blender or press through a sieve and pour over seafood.

Cook on medium heat for 5-7 minutes.

Boil pasta in salted water until al dente, then drain.

Serve the Marinara sauce over the pasta with green salad and crusty bread.

This is very quick to prepare and looks and tastes so professional, as though you've been at home all day, preparing.

Spanish Squid and Chorizo

olive oil
1 onion, diced
2 chorizo sausages
500 g squid (pineapple cut or rings)
2 cloves garlic, chopped
1 teaspoon sweet smoked Spanish paprika
1/2 cup dry sherry or dry white wine
400-g can of chopped tomatoes
To Serve
1/4 cup fresh flat-leafed parsley, chopped
Crusty bread

Heat oil in a large frying pan. Fry sliced chorizo and onion for 3-4 minutes until lightly brown.

Remove to one side, and fry squid in 2 batches.

Add chorizo, onion, garlic, and paprika.

Cook for 1 minute more. Add sherry to the pan, and reduce for 2-3 minutes.

Add tomatoes and simmer for 5 minutes until sauce thickens. Season with salt and pepper.

Scatter with parsley, and serve with crusty bread on the side to soak up the juices.

This can be made in 20 minutes as squid and chorizo cook quickly.

Smoked-Salmon Salad

fillet of smoked salmon
baby spinach leaves
freshly ground black pepper
juice of 1 lime or lemon
feta cheese
1 can of whole baby beetroot

Dressing
juice and zest of 1 lime
1/2 teaspoon salt
1 tablespoon olive oil

To Decorate
1 avocado, peeled, stoned, sliced, and squeezed
with lemon juice to stop browning
1/4 cup pumpkin seeds

Place baby spinach leaves on a serving dish.

Diana Johnson

Place a fillet of smoked salmon on top.

Season with pepper and lime juice.

Add cubes of feta cheese and halved baby beetroot.

Decorate with slices of avocado and pumpkin seeds.

Sweet-and-Sour Fish

500 g boneless fish fillets (i.e. blue cod)

Coating
1/2 teaspoon salt
1/2 teaspoon celery salt
1/2 teaspoon onion salt
1 teaspoon of water
1 egg whisked with a fork
1 cup dry breadcrumbs

Sweet-and-Sour Sauce
2 tablespoons cornflour
1/2 cup sugar
1 tablespoon soya sauce
3 tablespoons oil
1/4 cup vinegar
1 cup water

To Serve
Hot cooked rice
Chopped spring onions

To make the coating, mix together the salts with one teaspoon of water, and add to egg.

Sauce

Mix cornflour, sugar, soya sauce, oil, vinegar and water together in a medium saucepan. Bring to the boil, stirring constantly, and reduce to a very low heat while cooking the fish.

Cut fish into fingers and dip into seasoned egg.

Place breadcrumbs in a plastic or paper bag. Shake the fish pieces, a few at a time to thoroughly coat in breadcrumbs before frying in hot oil until golden brown. Do not overcook. Drain on kitchen paper.

Serve on hot, cooked, long-grain rice. Pour hot sauce over fish. Sprinkle with chopped spring onions.

Serves 4-5.

Trout with Spinach and Hollandaise Sauce

1 x 2 kg trout
butter for greasing baking dish
juice of 2 lemons
2 tablespoons sherry
salt and pepper
6 bunches of spinach leaves

To Serve
Green salad
New potatoes
Hollandaise Sauce

Preheat oven to 180 °C. Fillet the trout, but leave the skin on. (Remove fine bones with tweezers.)

Diana Johnson

Butter a baking dish, and lay the trout fillets in the base. Drizzle the lemon juice and sherry over the fish, and season with salt and pepper.

Leave to marinate for 15 minutes. Bake in the oven for 20 minutes.

Wash the spinach, slice into small pieces, and cook in the microwave for 5 minutes.

To serve, place fillets on warmed serving plates or a platter, leaving the skin behind. Cover each fillet with a layer of spinach, and spoon hollandaise sauce over them.

New potatoes and a crisp green salad will go well with this dish.

One 2-kilogram trout will feed 4 hungry adults.

If you are in an area where you can catch your own trout, this is a great way to feed you and your guests.

Check with the local fishing shop for areas that can be fished during your holiday. Not only will you help preserve the trout population, but the fishing guide will advise you of the best areas to fish and the best lures to use.

Hollandaise Sauce
(microwave)

1 tablespoon lemon juice
2 egg yolks
50 g butter
1/4 cup cream
1/2 teaspoon dry mustard
1/4 teaspoon salt

Melt butter in the microwave on high heat for 30 seconds.

Add lemon juice, egg yolks, and cream.

Microwave on high heat for 1 minute, stirring after 30 seconds.

Add seasonings, and beat until smooth.

This sauce can be served with asparagus, broccoli, or fish.

Prawn Biryani
(microwave)

115 g prawns
2 teaspoons curry powder
1 tablespoon fresh chopped coriander
Juice of 1 lemon (2 tablespoons juice)
1/4 onion, finely chopped
1 clove garlic, finely chopped or crushed
2 teaspoons oil
1/3 cup long-grain rice
1 1/4 cups boiling stock or liquid
6 medium-sized mushrooms, sliced
1/2 cup frozen peas

To Garnish
Chopped coriander leaves
Low fat yogurt

Place prawns in a dish, and sprinkle with 1 teaspoon of the curry powder, coriander, and lemon juice. Set aside to marinate.

Place onion, oil, and garlic in a microwave bowl, and cook on high heat for 1 minute.

Add the remaining curry powder. Cook for one minute.

Add the rice and 1 cup of boiling stock. Cook on high heat for 4 minutes, stirring twice.

Add mushrooms and cook for 1 minute on high heat, stirring halfway through.

Add the prawns and remaining stock. Cook on high heat for 2 minutes.

Add peas, stir well, and cook for 2 minutes.

Serve garnished with coriander and low-fat yogurt.

Hot-Salmon-and-Broccoli Salad with Chive-and-Mustard Dressing

750 g new potatoes, cooked in salted water until tender (cut large ones into smaller pieces)
350 g broccoli, cut into florets and steamed for 5 minutes until tender
1 courgette, cut into thin strips (with a vegetable peeler)
1 small red onion, finely sliced

Dressing
1/2 lemon, juice and grated zest
2 tablespoons red wine vinegar
6 tablespoons olive oil
1 teaspoon wholegrain mustard
pinch of sugar
2 tablespoons chopped chives
1 small garlic clove, crushed
1 teaspoon wasabi powder
1/2 teaspoon coarse salt

Garnish
A few basil leaves

Whisk all dressing ingredients together. Season and set aside.

Place on to a serving platter the cooked potatoes, the steamed broccoli, the sliced courgette and finely sliced red onion and mix together.

Heat 1 tablespoon olive oil in a non-stick frying pan until searing hot.

Fry the salmon fillets for 2-3 minutes each side and flake the salmon.

Top the salad with the flaked salmon and sprinkle with a few torn basil leaves. Drizzle the dressing over the salad.

This salad serves 4.

Creamy Salmon and Sugar Snap Peas with Pasta

400 g fusilli pasta

150 g sugar snap peas, halved lengthwise

2 salmon steaks (300 g) or hot smoked salmon
or trout, adding a sprinkling of dill

Dressing

zest and juice of 1/2 lemon
4 tablespoons reduced fat crème fraîche

100 g rocket

Boil pasta, adding sugar snaps to the water 2 minutes before cooking time is up.

Drain and rinse under cold running water and drain again.

Salmon can be steamed over the pasta pan for about 7 minutes if you have a steamer basket or can be put on to a heatproof plate and microwaved on high for 2-3 minutes until fish flakes easily. Peel away any skin and break into large flakes and allow to cool.

For the dressing, mix lemon juice, zest, and crème fraîche. Season to taste.

(A few tablespoons of cold water can be added to make the consistency of double cream.

Toss pasta, peas, and rocket with the dressing. Flake and add salmon. Gently fold to combine.

This can be eaten warm or cold.

SALADS AND VEGETABLE DISHES

Smoked-Chicken Salad with Apricots or Mandarins

Dressing
250 g light sour cream
4 tablespoons lemon juice
ground pepper
2 teaspoons seedy mustard

1 kg smoked chicken, fat and skin removed,
cut into small pieces
1 can apricots, drained and chopped (or
1 can mandarin slices, drained)
1/4 cup of chopped spring onions
lettuce cups

For the dressing, mix together sour cream, lemon juice, pepper, and seedy mustard.

When ready to serve, place chicken into a bowl. Pour the dressing over, and fold in onions and chopped apricots or mandarins.

Serve in lettuce cups.

Smoked-Chicken-and-Rocket Salad

1 Lebanese cucumber, cut into strips with a vegetable peeler
2 1/2 cups smoked chicken, shredded
4 cups rocket leaves

1 sliced red onion

Dressing
2 tablespoons French herb dressing

Garnish
lime or lemon slices
baby herbs

To Serve
Sourdough bread, sliced and toasted

Toss together the cucumber, smoked chicken, rocket leaves, and red onion.

To serve, dress with French dressing, and serve on toasted, sourdough bread slices.

Garnish with lime or lemon slices and baby herbs.

Warm-Honey-and-Lamb Salad

500 g lamb fillets
2 tomatoes, cut into wedges
carrots shredded, red onions sliced, bean sprouts,
torn lettuce leaves (total of 6 cups)

Dressing
1 tablespoon olive oil
2 tablespoons honey
1 tablespoon fresh lime juice
To Serve
Lime wedges

Season lamb fillets, and sear in a non-stick pan for 4-5 minutes. Let stand for 5 minutes, and then slice.

In a bowl, combine carrots, red onions, bean sprouts, and lettuce leaves. Add the lamb and tomatoes.

For the dressing, combine olive oil, honey, and fresh lime juice.

Drizzle the dressing over the salad, and toss to combine.

Serve with lime wedges.

This serves 4. Time: 20 minutes.

Bean Salad

1 cup sugar
1 cup brown vinegar
1 cup water
1 can red kidney beans
1 can chickpeas
1 can cut baby corn cobs
1 can mixed beans
1/2 chopped onion
1/2 green pepper chopped

Boil together sugar, vinegar, and water for 10 minutes. Set aside to cool.

In a large bowl, mix together beans, chickpeas, corn cobs, mixed beans, onion and green pepper.

Pour cooled liquid over bean mixture. This will keep well in the fridge or will freeze well.

Diana Johnson

Caprese Salad

3 large ripe tomatoes, sliced
6-9 fresh basil leaves
100 g buffalo mozzarella, sliced

Alternate slices of tomatoes and cheese. Sprinkle with basil leaves.

Drizzle with extra-virgin olive oil and balsamic vinegar.

Pear, Date, Blue Cheese, and Walnut Salad with Rocket-and-Pinot-Noir Dressing

6 peeled and sliced pears
rocket or other salad greens
4 dates, chopped
6 walnuts, chopped
small blue cheese

Dressing
3/4 cup Pinot Noir
1 1/2 tablespoons liquid honey
1 1/2 tablespoons extra-virgin olive oil

For the dressing, in a saucepan, add Pinot Noir, honey, and olive oil. Bring to the boil and cool.

Arrange pears over a bed of rocket.

Add chopped dates and walnuts, and crumble the cheese over it.

Serve with dressing.

Coleslaw

1/4 cabbage, finely sliced
2 medium carrots, grated
1/2 onion, finely chopped
1-2 sticks celery, sliced finely
1/2 cup sultanas soaked in orange juice for 30 minutes
1/2 cup chopped mixed nuts

Dressing
1/2 cup mayonnaise
1/4 cup peanut butter
1/2 cup sour cream

Toss together the cabbage, carrots, onion, celery, sultanas, and nuts.

In a separate bowl, mix together mayonnaise, peanut butter, and sour cream.

Stir through coleslaw just before serving.

Italian Pasta Salad

2 cups shell pasta or similar
1 can chickpeas, drained and rinsed
1/2 chopped red onion
1/2 cup Kalamata olives, stones removed
1/2 cup cherry tomatoes
250 g ricotta cheese
handful of basil leaves

Dressing
1/4 cup white wine vinegar
3/4 cup virgin olive oil

53

1 tablespoon Dijon mustard
2 cloves garlic, pressed

Boil pasta in salted water until al dente.

Rinse in cold water, and place in a large bowl.

Add chickpeas, red onion, olives, tomatoes, ricotta cheese, and basil leaves.

For the dressing, mix together, in a screw-top jar, the wine vinegar, olive oil, mustard, and garlic.

Fold through the pasta salad just before serving.

Peppered Peach or Nectarine Salad with Chicken

1 1/2 tablespoons cider vinegar
1/2 cup olive oil
1 tablespoon freshly ground pepper
4 ripe, medium-sized freestone peaches or
nectarines, skinned, stoned and sliced
50 g baby spinach leaves
50 g rocket leaves
1 1/2 cups chicken, roasted, boned, and shredded
1 Lebanese cucumber, chopped coarsely

Mix vinegar, olive oil, pepper, and sliced peaches or nectarines together.

Toss lightly to coat peaches or nectarines.

Arrange the spinach and rocket leaves on a platter, and add the chicken, dressed peaches, and cucumber.

Serve with a little sea salt.

DRESSINGS

French Dressing

1 cup extra-virgin olive oil
1/2 cup cider vinegar or wine vinegar or balsamic vinegar
squeeze of lemon juice
1 teaspoon Dijon mustard
1 garlic clove, crushed
salt and pepper
fresh herbs (optional)

Mix ingredients in a screw-top jar, and shake before using.

Fresh, chopped herbs can be added.

Mayonnaise

1 can sweetened condensed milk
1/2 can malt vinegar
1/2 can cold, drinking water
1 teaspoon dry mustard
1/2 teaspoon salt

Empty condensed milk into a bowl, add vinegar, and water and stir well.

Mix mustard and salt with the remaining condensed milk in the can and add a little boiling water to dissolve.

Diana Johnson

Add to the vinegar, water, and condensed milk. Stir until mixed thoroughly. Extra vinegar or water can be added when needed to thin the mayonnaise.

This keeps well in the fridge in a covered container.

This is an old but very simple one and can be used alone or as base for other dressings. It keeps well.

Lemon Aioli

3 egg yolks
grated zest of 1 lemon
juice of 2 lemons
1 tablespoon wine vinegar
1 teaspoon brown sugar
1 cup extra-virgin olive oil (or try extra-virgin avocado oil)
salt and pepper to taste

Place egg yolks, lemon juice, vinegar, and sugar into a liquidizer, and whizz together.

Add oil slowly, blending until it forms a smooth dressing. Season with salt and pepper. Add grated lemon zest, and mix to combine. Refrigerate until required.

This can be used as a sauce with barbecued chicken or seafood or as a dressing for salads.

DESSERTS

Pressed Peaches or Nectarines

6 large free-stone peaches or nectarines
juice of 1 lemon
½ cup sugar

To Serve
Yogurt, cream or ice-cream

Peel, stone, and cut up fresh peaches or nectarines (freestone varieties are best). Place into a bowl in layers, sprinkling each layer with lemon juice and sugar.

Cover with cling wrap and a small plate, putting a weight on top. (A can of fruit is ideal). Leave for a few hours before serving with yogurt, cream or ice cream.

Chocolate Mousse

3 egg yolks
250 g chopped chocolate
300 mls cream

Topping
whipped cream
fresh raspberries
grated chocolate

Diana Johnson

Melt the chopped chocolate in a stainless-steel bowl over a pot of boiling water, making sure that the underside of the bowl is not touching the water.

Remove from the heat, and mix in cream. Whisk in egg yolks, and pour into cups.

Allow to set in the fridge for 2 hours.

Top with whipped cream, fresh raspberries, and grated chocolate.

Cherry Clafoutis

2 x 425-g cans black cherries or any well-drained, stewed, or canned fruit

Topping
2/3 cup plain flour
1/4 cup sugar
3 eggs
1 3/4 cups milk

To Serve
Icing sugar
Cream or ice cream

Grease a 25 cm, round flan dish. Drain cherries or fruit, and spoon over the base of the dish.

For the topping, sift the flour into a bowl, stir in the sugar and eggs and gradually stir in milk. Mix or blend until smooth.

Pour into the dish over the back of a spoon and over the fruit.

Place in the oven and bake at 175 °C for approximately 40 minutes or until brown and set.

Serve warm and dusted with icing sugar and with cream or ice cream.

This serves 4-6.

Clafoutis can be made up to one day ahead.

Banana Ice Cream

4 ripe bananas, sliced thinly and frozen in
a single layer on baking paper
1/2 cup unsweetened almond milk
1 teaspoon vanilla
2 tablespoons maple syrup

Topping
1/4 cup finely chopped toasted almonds
2 teaspoons maple syrup
pinch of coarse sea salt

For the topping, mix together the toasted almonds, maple syrup and sea salt.

Combine frozen bananas, almond milk, vanilla, and 2 tablespoons maple syrup, and pulse until the consistency of frozen cream.

Spoon into individual bowls and sprinkle the almond mixture over the banana ice cream.

Passion-Fruit-and-Coconut Pudding

1 cup desiccated coconut
3/4 cup caster sugar
1/2 cup plain flour
4 eggs
1 1/3 cups milk
125 g butter, melted and cooled
1/2 cup passion fruit pulp
1 tablespoon fresh lemon juice

To Serve
icing sugar to dust
strawberries

Preheat oven to 180 °C. Grease a 23-centimetre flan dish.

Combine coconut, sugar, and flour in a large bowl.

In a separate, medium bowl, combine eggs, milk, butter, passion fruit pulp, and lemon juice. Combine with dry ingredients. Pour the mixture into the flan dish.

Bake for 40 minutes or until pudding is lightly golden and just set.

Serve warm or at room temperature, dust with icing sugar and top with strawberries.

Swedish Platter Pancakes

1 1/4 cups flour
1/4 teaspoon salt
2 tablespoons sugar
2 eggs

2 1/4 cups milk
2 tablespoons melted butter

To Serve
berry jam
Icing sugar

cream or ice cream or yogurt

Sift flour and salt, and stir in sugar, eggs, and milk.

Mix in melted butter.

Heat pan and grease with a little butter.

Spread 2 tablespoons batter as thinly as possible in the pan.

Turn the pancake over and cook the other side.

Stack the cooked pancakes on top of one another.

When ready to serve, spread berry jam on each pancake, stack and dust with icing sugar. Cut into wedges and serve with cream or ice cream.

Crème Caramel
(microwave)

1/2 cup caster sugar
1 tablespoon water
700 mls milk
additional 1/2 cup caster sugar
grated rind of one orange
1 teaspoon vanilla essence

4 eggs
4 egg yolks
3 tablespoons orange liqueur

To Serve
Pouring cream

Place first measure of sugar and water in a heatproof glass bowl (1 1/2 litres). A fluted 23-centimetre Pyrex dish is ideal.

Cook for 4-5 minutes until liquid is a golden colour.

Swirl syrup to coat sides a little. Leave aside to cool.

In a separate microwave bowl, heat milk in the microwave with second measure of sugar, essence, and orange rind for 6 minutes until very hot but not boiling.

Whisk together eggs and yolks. Strain into hot milk mixture, and stir in liqueur. Pour carefully over the back of a spoon over the caramel.

Cook on 30 per cent heat or defrost setting for approximately 45 minutes until the custard is beginning to firm in the middle.

Chill well before turning out on to a flat serving dish.

Accompany with pouring cream.

Microwave Steamed Pudding with Dates or Mixed Dried Fruit

125 g butter
2 tablespoons golden syrup
1 tablespoon brown sugar

250 g chopped dates or mixed dried fruit
1 teaspoon baking soda
250 mls milk
1 cup self-raising flour
1/2 teaspoon cinnamon
1/2 teaspoon ground ginger

In a medium size microwave bowl, melt butter, syrup, and brown sugar on high heat for 1 1/2-2 minutes.

Add dried fruit or dates and soda dissolved in milk.

Stir in sifted dry ingredients.

Microwave on high heat for 1 minute, stirring after each 30 seconds. Spoon into a greased microwave-proof bowl, and cover with cling wrap. Microwave on high heat for 3 minutes. Reduce to medium heat, and cook for a further 5 1/2 minutes.

Allow to stand for 5 minutes before serving.

Serve with ice cream or custard (or both).

Christmas Pudding
(microwave)

4 slices of bread, crusts removed and finely crumbed,
soaked in 4 tablespoons brandy
125 g butter
125 g brown sugar
pinch of salt
3 eggs, beaten
375 g mixed dried fruit, dates included
50 g blanched almonds

1/4 teaspoon nutmeg
1/4 teaspoon mixed spice
1/2 teaspoon ground ginger
1/2 teaspoon sodium bicarbonate
60 g plain flour

Soak breadcrumbs in brandy.

In a separate bowl, cream butter, salt, and sugar.

Add eggs and mix in bread and brandy.

Sift together nutmeg, mixed spice, ground ginger, baking soda and flour.

Into the creamed butter and sugar, fold in fruit and almonds alternately with sifted dry ingredients.

Spoon into a greased 17-centimetre pudding-shaped microwave bowl lined with cling wrap.

Cover with cling wrap. Microwave on medium heat for 7 minutes.

Reduce to low heat for a further 8 minutes. Turn out on to foil, and completely enclose until cold.

To reheat, place on a serving plate. Cover with cling wrap, and microwave on high heat for 3 minutes. Serve with custard or brandy sauce.

Pancakes

1 1/4 cups flour
3 teaspoons baking powder
1 tablespoon sugar
1/2 teaspoon salt

1 beaten egg
1 cup milk
2 tablespoons vegetable oil

Sift flour, baking powder, and salt. Stir in sugar.

In a separate bowl, combine egg, milk, and oil.

Add to dry ingredients and stir until just combined. The batter will be lumpy.

Cook on a hot non-stick frying pan in 8-centimetre rounds until bubbles begin to burst.

Turn over and cook until golden brown.

As a suggestion, any of the following can be added to the mixture before cooking:

2 tablespoons blueberries
Or 1/2 cup of well-drained crushed pineapple
Or 1 mashed banana

CAKES

Frangipane Tarts

6 individual ready-made pastry cases
100 g butter, softened
100 g sugar
100 g almond meal
1 egg
1 teaspoon vanilla essence
grated rind of 1/2 orange
berry or fruit jam

Mix together butter, sugar, almond meal, egg, vanilla, and grated orange rind.

Place 1 teaspoon jam then 1 dessertspoon almond mix then 1 teaspoon jam then 1 dessertspoon almond mix into each pastry case.

Bake in the oven for 18 minutes at 180 °C.

Lime Syrup Cupcakes

125 g unsalted butter
3 eggs
200 mls milk
1 3/4 cups self-raising flour
2 cups caster sugar
2 1/3 cups desiccated coconut
zest and juice of 6 limes or 4 lemons
melted butter for greasing
plain flour for dusting

Preheat oven to 170 °C. Grease 8 ovenproof coffee mugs with butter, and dust with flour. Melt unsalted butter in a small pan over low heat, and set aside to cool slightly.

Whisk in eggs and milk.

Combine flour, 1 1/2 cups of sugar, coconut, and zest in a large bowl. Add melted butter, and mix until smooth. Spoon mixture into prepared cups.

Bake for 25 minutes or until cooked when tested with a skewer. Remove from the oven, and pierce the tops with a skewer.

Place lime or lemon juice and the remaining sugar into a small pan, and bring to the boil over low heat. Cook until mixture thickens slightly.

Pour syrup over the cakes. Cool slightly, and serve.

CAKES AND BISCUITS
TO TAKE WITH YOU

Sultana and Cherry Cake

250 g butter
1 cup sugar
3 eggs
2 cups flour
1 teaspoon baking powder
150g glace cherries
1 cup sultanas

Cover sultanas with water, bring to the boil, then drain.

Allow to cool, and add 150 grams glacé cherries.

Preheat oven to 170 °C.

Line the base of a 22-centimetre round cake tin with baking paper.

Cream butter and sugar until creamy and fluffy.

Beat in eggs one at a time.

Sift and fold in flour and baking powder.

Fold in the cooled sultanas and cherries, and pour mixture into prepared tin.

Bake for 60-65 minutes until skewer comes out clean. Turn out and cool on a wire rack.

Remove baking paper.

Nutty Fruit Cake

3/4 cup plain flour
1/2 teaspoon baking powder
650 g mixed dried fruit
200 g mixed raw nuts
3/4 cup firmly packed brown sugar
3 eggs, lightly whisked
1 teaspoon vanilla essence

Preheat oven to 160 °C.

Grease a 21centimetre x 10-centimetre loaf tin, and line with baking paper.

Sift flour and baking powder into a bowl. Stir in mixed fruit, nuts, and sugar.

Add eggs and essence, and stir to combine. Spoon mixture into a prepared pan.

Bake for 1 1/2 hours or until skewer inserted into the centre comes out clean.

Allow to stand for 15 minutes. Transfer to wire rack to cool.

This is best left un-iced.

This cake is an ideal Christmas cake.

Diana Johnson

Biscotti

2 cups sugar
4 cups flour
1 tablespoon baking powder
100 g dates
100 g glacé cherries
100 g hazel nuts
100 g pistachio nuts
100 g whole almonds
100 g sultanas
zest of 2 lemons
6 eggs

Mix all ingredients until rolling consistency is achieved.

Flour the board, and flour your hands.

Take 2 handfuls, and roll them into a long roll (approximately 2 centimetres in diameter).

Place on a non-stick baking tray or baking paper on a tray, and flatten the top. Repeat leaving space between rolls.

Bake at 180 °C for 15 to 20 minutes.

Slice diagonally into 1-centimetre slices. Place back on the tray.

Bake for 10 minutes at 140 °C.

Remove from the oven, turn biscotti over, and bake for 5 minutes more.

Biscotti keep well in an airtight container so are especially good for taking on holiday.

PICNICS AND BARBEQUES

A picnic needs fresh crusty bread. Make your own or there will be a great variety available from supermarkets and bakeries, and lots of fresh ingredients to satisfy everyone's tastes. Include tomatoes, cucumber, ham or salamis, cooked chicken broken into pieces, gherkins, bread and butter pickles, olives, prawns in cocktail sauce, washed lettuce leaves, quiche, asparagus or prawn rolls, and frittata.

When cooking on the barbecue, remove all fat from chops or meat before grilling to avoid fires, charred food, and a fatty mess to be cleaned up.

Use pre-cooked sausages, or boil your favourite sausages to remove any fat before placing them on the barbecue. This also ensures that they are thoroughly cooked.

Use mixed herbs or ground-powder type seasoning to sprinkle on the meat or vegetables before cooking rather than marinades as they tend to burn on to the barbecue and spoil the flavour of your food.

After you've finished with the barbeque, leave it turned on high heat for 5 minutes to burn off any remnants of food and assist in cleaning. Scrape the barbeque with scraper and clean it with a paper towel to be ready for the next use.

Spiced Lamb Skewers with Harissa Yogurt

2 tablespoons smoked paprika
1 tablespoon ground coriander
2 teaspoons ground cumin
2 tablespoons olive oil
1 teaspoon sea salt
1 teaspoon cracked pepper
1 kg diced lamb
2 red capsicums, cut into 2 cm dice
1 cup Greek-style yogurt
1 tablespoon harissa paste

71

Diana Johnson

1 tablespoon fresh coriander leaves
salt to season
16 bamboo skewers soaked in water for at least an hour

Place paprika, coriander, cumin, and olive oil into a large glass or ceramic dish. Season with salt and pepper and add diced lamb. Toss to coat. Cover and refrigerate for 30 minutes. Thread diced lamb and red capsicum alternately on to 16 bamboo skewers. Heat chargrill pan or barbecue grill to medium-high heat.

Cook skewers for 5-7 minutes, turning during cooking.

For the harissa yogurt, place Greek-style yogurt in a bowl. Add harissa paste and fresh coriander. Season with salt, and stir to combine.

Time to prepare is 30 minutes plus 30 minutes to marinate the meat.

WINTER SOUPS

These are great, hearty soups on a cold day or night and will satisfy even the hungriest skier.

Mushroom Soup with Blue Cheese

½ kg button mushrooms sliced
2 packets mushroom soup mix made with milk
250g blue vein cheese
Black pepper
Chopped fresh herbs (coriander, parsley and chives)

To Serve
Plain yogurt
Crusty bread

Chop 1/2 kg button mushrooms, and fry in a little butter and olive oil.

Make up 2 packets mushroom soup mix with milk, and cook as instructed on the packet. Add the fried mushrooms.

When cooked, place the soup mixture together with the blue-vein cheese into a food processor and process together.

Add black pepper and fresh herbs. Keep warm on low heat but don't allow to boil.

Swirl plain yogurt on top, and serve with crusty bread.

Diana Johnson

Minestrone Soup
(microwave)

1 medium onion, chopped
1 clove garlic, chopped
1/2 cup celery, chopped
1/4 cup capsicum, chopped
1 tablespoon olive oil
a pinch of oregano
1/2 teaspoon sugar
1/4 teaspoon white pepper
440-g can kidney beans
440-g can chopped tomatoes
1 medium zucchini, diced
1/4 cup white rice
3 cups stock
1/4 cup red wine
1 tablespoon chopped parsley

To Serve
Extra chopped parsley
Grated parmesan cheese

Place in a 3-litre microwave casserole the onion, garlic, celery, and chopped capsicum with 1 tablespoon oil.

Cover and cook on high heat for 6 minutes.

Add oregano, sugar, pepper, beans, tomatoes, zucchini, white rice, stock, red wine, and parsley.

Cover and cook on high heat for 20 minutes stirring 3 times during cooking.

Sprinkle with extra parsley and grated Parmesan.

Mulligatawny Soup
(microwave)

60 g butter
1-litre brown stock
1 large onion, chopped
1 clove garlic, crushed and chopped
1 apple, peeled and chopped
1/2 cup flour
2 tablespoons fruit chutney
2 teaspoons curry powder
salt to taste
1 tablespoon tomato paste
½ cup cooked rice
1 tablespoon chopped parsley

Place butter, onion, and garlic in a 2-litre casserole. Cook on high heat for 6 minutes. Blend in flour and curry powder, and cook for another minute. Add tomato paste and stock, and cook on high heat for 15 minutes (or until boiling). Stir in apple, chutney, and salt. Puree in food processor. Correct the seasoning. Cook to reheat for 5 minutes. Fold in the cooked rice and parsley.

Mushroom Soup

300 g fresh mushrooms sliced
1 brown onion, peeled and chopped
1 clove of garlic, crushed and chopped finely
1 tablespoon soya sauce
2 tablespoons flour
1 packet of mushroom soup
2 litres water

2 teaspoons stock powder
2 tablespoons oil or a mixture of oil and butter
salt and pepper

To serve

sour cream

In a large saucepan, add oil (and butter, if using). Fry the onion, garlic, and mushroom for 3 minutes, stirring frequently. Add flour, continuing to stir, but don't allow to brown. Mix together the stock powder and water, and gradually stir into the mixture until it thickens. Stir continuously so that no lumps form. Add soya sauce and packet of mushroom soup. Cook further for 3 minutes. Serve with 1 tablespoon sour cream with each serving.

Seafood Chowder

2 tablespoons olive oil
150 g rindless bacon, chopped
1 onion, sliced
1 stick celery, diced
2 cloves garlic, chopped
2 medium-sized waxy potatoes, peeled and chopped
400-g can of chopped tomatoes
400 g white-fleshed fish fillets, cubed
12 cockles, scrubbed (optional)
150 g each raw prawns and scallops
salt and freshly ground black pepper
2 tablespoons chopped fresh parsley

Heat oil in heavy-based saucepan.

Add bacon, onion, garlic, and celery.

Fry gently for 10 minutes, stirring regularly until vegetables are soft.

Add potatoes, tomatoes, and 3 cups cold water.

Bring to the boil, reduce heat, and simmer for 10 minutes.

Add seafood and simmer for 5-10 minutes or until seafood is just cooked.

Season chowder with salt and pepper to taste.

Serve sprinkled with parsley.

DRINKS

Iced Coffee

1 can sweetened condensed milk
2 tablespoons instant coffee, dissolved in a little hot water
4 cans drinking water
3 cans milk
a pinch of salt
2 drops vanilla

Mix all together in a large bowl. Cover and store in the fridge.

This iced coffee is a great favourite.

Citrus Cordial

2 large oranges
2 large lemons
6 cups sugar
6 cups boiling water
2 tablespoons citric acid

Cut the unpeeled fruit into rough chunks and process in a food processor or kitchen whizz.

Place fruit into a large bowl, and cover with sugar. Add boiling water and stir until dissolved and allow to cool.

Stir in citric acid, and leave for 24 hours.

Strain into sterilized bottles.

Glass bottles with screw tops are best. To sterilize, wash in warm, soapy water, rinse, and put on a tray in a cold oven.

Turn oven on to 110 °C. When it reaches 110 °C, turn it off. Leave bottles in the oven for 10 minutes. To sterilize caps, boil for a few minutes in a saucepan.

Make sure they are dry before using.

This cordial will keep up to 12 months and is ideal to take with you.

Coffee or Chocolate Almond Milk

2 sliced bananas, frozen
1-litre carton almond milk
2 heaped teaspoons instant coffee or drinking chocolate, dissolved in 1 tablespoon boiling water
1/2 teaspoon nutmeg
1/2 teaspoon cinnamon
6-8 ice cubes

Process all together in a kitchen whizz and serve.

Refreshing Lunchtime Drink (non-alcoholic)

1/2 cup pomegranate juice
1 large bottle ginger ale

Mix pomegranate juice and ginger ale, and serve over ice.

Diana Johnson

Holidays are to have fun but take care.

If it's sunny, either winter or summer, the sun can burn, so wear hats with brims and use sunblock and cover shoulders, especially the little ones' delicate skins.

If you're on the water, life jackets are essential.

If you're hiking over the mountains, even if the weather is clear and sunny when you set off, be prepared with warm clothing and extra food, and make sure that you tell someone where you're going and when to expect you back.

Do contact them as soon as you return or if you change your plans.

Drive carefully.

Winter roads can be treacherous, so check the road conditions before you leave.

Check the forecast every day, and if snow is forecast, put your vehicle where you will be able to easily move it the following day.

Take chains with you and make sure you know how to fit them. For front-wheel drive vehicles, the chains need to be fitted to the front wheels, and if it's a rear-wheel drive, fit them to the rear wheels.

Ski areas can be frosty. To remove frost from your vehicle, scrape the windscreen, rear window, and side windows with a credit card or similar. Use plastic as it won't leave permanent scratches on the glass.

Using water to defrost your windscreen can cause a dangerous frozen puddle beside your car and water can freeze the locks.

Investing in a can of defrosting spray can be ideal and should be available from most petrol stations in the area.

Remember that if you are in a frost-prone area, temperatures can stay below freezing point for weeks and puddles can be treacherous.

Industrial salt can be sprinkled on steps and pathways to thaw out frozen areas.

If you are holidaying in a tourist area, watch all traffic and expect the worst driving as many of them are visitors driving on unfamiliar roads, on a different side of the road from home, or they can just be gazing at the beautiful scenery.

Be forgiving as a panicking driver can be even more of a problem.

I wish you all the holiday that you deserve and one that your family will remember and thank you for the rest of their lives.

Recipe Index

General Index

Diana Johnson

E

egg noodles   36
egg yolks   44-5, 56-8, 62
eggs   4-5, 11-12, 21-2, 28, 35, 42,
    58, 60-70

F

fettuccine   32
fish   5, 34, 37-9, 42-5, 48, 76
flour   3-4, 11-13, 16, 21-2, 58, 60-1,
    63-70, 75-6
  cornflour   18, 31, 35
  cornmeal flour   16
  self-raising flour   3-4, 11-13, 63, 66
  wholemeal flour   3
frittata   6, 11-12, 71

G

garlic   2, 6-8, 15-22, 26-30, 34,
    36-41, 45-6, 54-5, 74-6
ginger   8, 18, 24-5, 30, 34, 36,
    63-4, 79
ginger ale   79
gravy   22-3

H

ham   11-12, 71
honey   1, 9, 30, 33, 50-2

I

ice cream   57-9, 61, 63

J

juice:
  lemon   21-2, 24, 41, 44-6, 48-9,
    55-7, 60, 67
  lime   8-9, 16-17, 34, 42, 50-1
  pomegranate   79

K

kidney beans   20, 51, 74
  red   20, 51

L

lamb   50-1, 71-2
lemons   2, 5, 9-10, 17, 22, 26, 43,
    45, 47, 56-7, 66, 70, 78
lettuce   6, 50-1
limes   8-9, 16-17, 34, 41-2, 50-1,
    66-7

M

macaroni   33
mandarins   9, 25, 49
mayonnaise   5, 16-17, 33, 53, 55-6
meats   5, 71-2
milk   4, 12-13, 23, 58, 60-1, 63,
    65, 67, 73
  almond   59, 79
  condensed   55-6, 78
mint   26
mushroom soup   19, 73, 75
mushrooms   6-7, 11-12, 14, 19, 32,
    35, 45-6, 73, 75-6
mustard   5, 7, 15, 22-3, 28, 33, 44,
    46, 49, 54-5
  Dijon   22-3, 54-5
  wholegrain   33, 46

N

nectarines   2, 54, 57
noodles   18-19, 23-5, 31, 34, 36-7
  chicken   23
  ribbon   19
  rice   36
nuts   7, 23-6, 30, 53, 69
  cashew   23-4, 30

Edwards Brothers Malloy
Ann Arbor MI. USA
January 6, 2017